New York Hotel

Also by Ian Seed

Anonymous Intruder (Shearsman Books, 2009)
Shifting Registers (Shearsman Books, 2011)
Makers of Empty Dreams (Shearsman Books, 2014)
Identity Papers (Shearsman Books, 2016)

Chapbooks

Threadbare Fables (Like This Press, 2012)
Sleeping with the Ice Cream Vendor (Knives, Forks and Spoons Press, 2012)
Fidelities (Red Ceilings Press, 2015)

Translations

No One Else at Home
        (translated from the Polish of Joanna Skalska) (Flax, 2007)
the straw which comes apart
        (translated from the Italian of Ivano Fermini) (Oystercatcher Press, 2010)
The Thief of Talant
        (from the French of Pierre Reverdy) (Wakefield Press, 2016)

Fiction

Amore mio (Flaxebooks, 2010)
Italian Lessons (LikeThisPress, 2017)

Ian Seed

New York Hotel

Shearsman Books

First published in the United Kingdom in 2018 by
Shearsman Books
50 Westons Hill Drive
Emersons Green
BRISTOL
BS16 7DF

Shearsman Books Ltd Registered Office
30–31 St. James Place, Mangotsfield, Bristol BS16 9JB
(this address not for correspondence)

www.shearsman.com

ISBN 978-1-84861-572-4

ACKNOWLEDGEMENTS
Some of these poems have previously appeared in the following journals:
*Decals of Desire, The Café Irreal, Flash: the International Short-Short Story
Magazine, The Fortnightly Review, International Times, Poetry Salzburg
Review, Shearsman* and *Tears in the Fence.*

'Recall' was first published in the anthology *Over Land, Over Sea: Poems
for Those Seeking Refuge* (eds. Kathleen Bell, Emma Lee, Siobhan Logan,
Five Leaves Press, 2015).

'Left Open' was first published in *Nerve Damage* (ed. Rupert M Loydell,
Analogue Flashback Books, 2016). 'Smoke' was first published in *Black
Noise* (eds. Abigail Brookes, Ayesha Kinley, LikeThisPress, 2017).

Contents

3

4

'Am I not,
Myself, only half of a figure of a sort,

A figure half seen, or seen for a moment, a man
Of the mind, an apparition apparelled in

Apparels of such lightest look that a turn
Of my shoulder and quickly, too quickly, I am gone?'

—Wallace Stevens

I

Generation Gap

My maternal grandfather turned up at my council flat with his father, who was a tiny bearded man in an ancient wheelchair. I hadn't seen them for a long time. Without saying hello, my great grandfather raised a fist in the air and began to berate me for being nearly sixty and still without a proper home or job. Even when my grandfather lifted him out of the chair, carried him to the toilet and put him down on the seat, he continued to scold me. The whole flat soon started to stink, but I said nothing through fear of offending them.

Memory

When I was fourteen, my father returned to England after a decade abroad. I hoped he might have settled down now that he had a new wife. But she told me he spent most of the day wandering around his old house as if he were visiting a city he had never seen before, with his shirt tail hanging out, cardigan buttoned up in the wrong holes, marmalade on his trousers, and with the look of a lost boy in his eyes despite his thick greying beard, which I envied because I had still not started to shave.

Evolution

There were some large black ducks, not unlike dodos, by the German lake. I began pushing one gently by the beak until it pushed back and then slowly and clumsily chased me round and round. From nearby metal benches, some Germans looked on bemused.

We hadn't been here since my daughter was a toddler. At that time, she was frightened by the birds, and I had played the same game to amuse her. Now she was a teenager exploring the old town on her own, while my wife slept off her hangover. I had nothing better to do.

A German man, roughly the same age and height as me, but much broader in the shoulder, got up and started playing my game with one of the ducks. But he did so in an aggressive and exaggerated manner, as if to parody me. The others smiled and their eyes lit up, perhaps anticipating my inevitable humiliation.

Late

After Joseph Cornell

The palatial hotel is over a century old and retains its grand style. The wooden lift still sits in its steel cage. Leaving my suitcase with the porter, I go upstairs to say hello to my father, who has arrived earlier that day. But there is nobody in his room. I take the ancient lift again and go wandering from floor to floor. The search through ornate corridors is so pleasurable that I soon forget what it is I am looking for. One room has its door open. A woman as glamorous as a silent movie star is lying on the silk sheets of her bed. She blows me a kiss and beckons with her finger. I stand in her doorway, unable to move. Then she sneezes, and I hurry on my way. Eventually I find my father sitting at a table in a lounge on the top floor. He is staring at his watch while waving away a waiter in a white tuxedo. He looks disappointed when he spots me, as if he should have known all along I would only be up to my old tricks again.

Views

The old philosopher has not paid his hotel bill for as long as anyone can remember. On the rare occasion when one of the staff dares to broach the subject with him, he mutters under his breath, coughs, then walks away surprisingly briskly. He takes the ancient lift all the way up to the roof garden where he will spend hours gazing out over the vast bay, his eyes following one ship after another as it disappears over the horizon.

With me, the foreigner, it is a different story. My efforts to settle everything correctly only make the staff all the more suspicious. To avoid their stares, I spend my evenings down at the port. Here I can lean unnoticed against a smooth soapy wall and watch the fishermen and their families unload their haul in the light of the setting sun.

Soundproof

Due to a booking error, I found myself sharing a hotel room with a woman I'd never met before. She smiled at me as if it were the most natural thing in the world, and started to unpack her small suitcase, putting her clothes away neatly in a drawer. The situation was full of promise, I realised, but at that moment I needed the toilet.

The bathroom was tiny and the roof sloped so low, I had to stoop. It was as if I were trapped in a doll's house. It occurred to me that this woman, with her dark eye shadow and stiff dark hair, and black dress which clung to her curves, was no more than a doll.

When I returned to the bedroom, she was sitting on the side of the bed, pouring out two glasses of red wine. Through the window I could see a plane taking off from the nearby airport. It rose into the sky in complete silence because the window was sealed tight.

Interview

There were three of them at the round table where they invited me to sit: a young lecturer in psychology, a drama teacher, who happened to be his wife (a little older, dark hair in a bobtail, heavy eye shadow), and an ancient emeritus professor. The lecturer was saying something about the traumatic effect of marital breakdown on children. I nodded every now and again until his wife broke in: 'I doubt you really have any idea,' she said, 'of what it is truly like for the child.'

I wasn't sure whether she was addressing me or her husband, but I felt obliged to tell them of my own father's compulsive philandering, his bitter separation from my mother when I was eight, and her breakdown when he went to Italy and vanished there. Later I tried to find him, and ended up living for several years in Turin. Here I discovered and translated the books of Cesare Pavese, another philanderer, who wrote poems despairing of the possibility of ever being able to love and hanged himself in a hotel room.

The elderly professor maintained a ghostly silence, while the lecturer stared into his tea as if thinking about something else entirely. His wife must have been turned on by my story of suffering, for the whole time she kept giving me secretive glances and pressing her knee against my thigh under the table.

Early Promise

After my divorce and losing my job, I was reduced to wandering the streets and dossing in doorways. One day a man threw me some coins. I recognised him as a friend from my youth. Over the next few weeks, he put me up in his luxury apartment. He seemed to take pleasure in my dependence upon him, for in our younger days I had been the one with the brilliant future. Now he wanted me to keep him amused. He would take me to parties, dressing me up in one of his discarded suits, which was much too loose on my scrawny body. One night he came across an old lover, and abandoned me to make my own way back to his apartment through the dark streets of the city. Taking a path through a park, I got lost and decided to kip down on a bench.

When dawn came, I could see a small building that I recognised as the Italian café I frequented in my youth. Giovanni and Rosa had always been kind to me, treating me like the son they yearned for. It was in vain that I had tried to hide my crush on Rosa, for I couldn't help blushing whenever she spoke to me. I think Giovanni knew about this but was generous-hearted enough not to mind. He would always offer me an extra coffee on the house. It made his wife happy, he said, just to watch me stare dreamily into space or become lost in a book. It was the kind of thing they never had time for in their own lives. I wondered now if they were still alive, if they might still be there, and what they would say if I knocked on their door.

Returning Home

It was after midnight. I was walking down a snow-covered street past an old church, when the lighting went off, and I slipped, twisting my ankle. There was no one else around. If I called out, would anyone hear my cry? Would anyone have the courage to leave the warmth of their house? And if a stranger happened to pass, would he help me up or would he take advantage of my weakened condition to rob me by the steps of the church where I had fallen?

Interview with a Priest

His words were changing into a language I couldn't comprehend. At the same time, the hairs on his knuckles were growing into spikes. My stomach felt tender as a crocodile's, as if my falling on the spikes were inevitable.

A Man of Some Influence

I was meditating on the bed in a shoulder-stand position, the backs of my heels against floral wallpaper, my head, neck, shoulders and elbows on the pillow, my hands supporting my hips. A man in a tweed suit dashed into the room. He had a bald head and a beard like Lenin's, but his expression was mild and English. 'Oscar needs your help,' he said. By this he meant that Oscar Wilde, a good friend of mine, had been taken to court and needed me to testify on his behalf. I realised at that moment that I couldn't go, for my forehead had begun to swell drastically like a balloon. Instead of replying, I took my hands away from my hips, and, not without some sense of final satisfaction, began gently stroking and pressing the swelling with the tips of my fingers.

Historical

This was the tree where Charles as a young prince had once hidden during the English Civil War, but it looked as if it were made of plastic. The tree was certainly not a good enough reason to hang around, although that was what my girlfriend wanted to do, mainly because she was interested in some of the local merry-making men. Personally I'd had enough of their endless Heil Hitler jokes. They would use any excuse to click their heels, thrust their right arm forward, and shout something in what they thought was German. One of them had published an autobiography, the story of how through sheer fluke, he had been able to turn his life into a success. I was quite envious. It was little comfort that the book was badly written.

The New Therapy

Given my complicated history, I was sent to France for psycho-analysis. I thought my reading of Jung and my knowledge of French would stand me in good stead. When I arrived, I found the psychoanalytic institution occupied a shiny corporate build-ing. The receptionist at the entrance desk told me to wait while she called the analyst I had been assigned to. A few minutes later, a man with crew cut hair and dressed in a tight-fitting suit came towards me. He had a bulky, bull-like presence, yet his handshake was soft and clammy. As we went up in the lift to his office, he stood a little too close. In my uneasiness, I began to stammer in French, but he interrupted and told me not to bother: the new psychoanalytic institution was international; their working language was English.

Existentialist

Revisiting the city of my student days, I went into the multi-storey bookshop where I had once worked. I was surprised to see that it was full of antique and second-hand books instead of its previous glossy selection. Perhaps now it is trying to be more 'authentic', I thought, more about the love of literature than money. But the whole atmosphere was like that of a funeral. None of the booksellers laughed or joked anymore, and the shop was almost deserted. The new manager – who had previously worked for the Arts Council before being made redundant – ignored me as if my presence were a threat. By his side stood a plump, grey-haired woman. It took me a few moments to recognise her as the young assistant I had once had a crush on. 'We don't know what happens to us after our deaths,' she said to me, 'but we certainly won't be able to make love.' That evening I accepted the invitation to share her bed. I no longer desired her, but it was one way to defy the manager and his insistence on authenticity.

My Grandchildren Are Waiting

It's time to leave the biggest second-hand bookshop I have ever been to – but there's still so much to see. Right beside me are shelves and shelves of the novels of Dostoyevsky. Some I have never heard of, yet alone read. Even those I have read seem strange enough for me to want to return to. It has been such a long time. I want to see how much I remember, how much I have changed inside.

As of Old

When I had finished shopping, I went to visit the street where I used to live on the edge of the city. A man with long white hair rode up to me on an ancient bicycle. It took me a few moments to realise that he was a friend from my student days. I had lent him the bicycle years ago, and hadn't seen him since. As of old, I knew that he would ask for money he couldn't repay. In the meantime, he looked thirsty and tired, so I offered him a drink from the bottle of water in my hand. He drank until the bottle was empty. I went to buy another one from a bar I once frequented, while he waited with his bicycle in the shade of an overhanging balcony.

On the way back, I forgot the way and ended up taking a wrong turning. I found myself walking through mud at the back of a block of flats. The Italian shoes I had bought were soon filthy. How my friend would laugh when he saw me.

2

Inflated

When I stumbled upon the chain-smoking Italian poet who used to chat to me for hours on end, I wanted to pay him back for the ways in which he had enriched my youth. I went into an old-fashioned tobacconist's, where the Tunisian man behind the counter spoke fluent Italian with a Naples accent. He told me that my Italian was as good as his, though I spoke it in a 'scholastic' manner, like someone who had been taught. I assured him that I too had learnt the language as a young man in the cafes and streets, though I conceded that I had not been back to Italy for a long time. He smiled and handed over the three packets of cigarettes I asked for. When I saw how much they cost, I was astonished. Why did the poor poet choose to smoke such an expensive brand?

Apparatus

My friend Marie was ill with the same disease that had killed my father. I decided to go and visit her in Milan, where she scraped a living as a freelance English teacher. When I got to her one-room flat in the suburbs, the front door was ajar. Someone was coughing inside. I knocked gently and walked in. Marie wasn't there. Instead, there was a young man with a dark fringe, who was taking out a complicated-looking apparatus from a doctor's bag.

'Aha… you must be Marietta's friend from England,' he said, without looking at me. 'I have to go now and see my next patient. I'll show you how this works.'

He connected various tubes, pressed a number of keys in quick succession, and went through a series of instructions.

'There is no way I can remember all this,' I said, starting to panic. 'I've just had a long journey, you know.'

He repeated everything, but this time more rapidly and with a rising tone of impatience. Then, coughing and almost hurling the apparatus into my arms, he left.

Shortly afterwards, Marie arrived looking brisk and professional and not at all ill, unlike the last time I had seen her. She told me not to worry. She knew all there was to know from her own research. Indeed, it was she who had insisted on trying the apparatus; her doctor was quite ignorant.

'Why don't you give me the chance to get changed?' she said. 'You can take me out to dinner.'

That evening, as we took the metro into the city, I thought about the new cure. If only it had been available a few years ago, my father might be alive today. I could see him and tell him the story of my life.

Stay

Before we reached the city, the snow started to fall, and we were forced to spend most of the winter in a village in the forest. The local priest invited us to stay with him. To be courteous to our host, we attended church services several times a week, even though we were non-believers. The local congregation started to swell. Soon the services were packed, and the villagers pressed as close to us as they could. This was due to their fascination with our foreignness, the priest explained, and we should not be afraid. He lent us novels by Dostoyevsky to keep our minds occupied. When the snow finally melted away, we thanked the priest and set off once again. Within hours, we reached the edge of the forest. From there, we could see the sky reflected in the city's golden domes, much closer than we had thought.

Baptism

It had been a long journey. While I was waiting outside the chapel for the others to arrive, a woman asked me if I could look after her dog for a few minutes. After some time, she had still not returned. What, I wondered, was I going to do with this shaggy black creature she had left me with? I decided to go and look for her. The village was so small that I soon reached its edges. Here there was a river, and on the other side another chapel, similar to the first, but situated in a heathland of the softest green and purple hues I had ever seen. It felt familiar and yet like another world. I wanted to cross the river and touch the softness, but there was no bridge. Besides, the dog was starting to bark as if suddenly realising that I was not his real owner.

The Monastery

I entered the ancient park and saw monks strolling around in pairs, their heads bent close together as they talked. I climbed to the top of a hill. Just over the crest there was a scholar monk sitting on a swing. When he asked me what I wanted there, I told him I was interested in joining their order. He replied softly that years of study were required on my part before such an application could be considered. I felt now that I must in some way make him realise that in spite of my flippant, wanting-easy-kicks appearance I was capable of something much higher. Yet instead I told him childishly that I wasn't interested in his silly little garden of magic anyway. Before he could reply, I spun around on one heel, and began striding in the direction of the woods where the monastery lay. To enter was, I knew, by custom forbidden. But I also knew that the monks were physically powerless to stop me.

Travelling Salesman

The building had once been a grand cathedral, but now only a small part of it was used for religious purposes. At the end of a long corridor, I was given a room for the night. In medieval times it had operated as a monk's cell. The door was made up of a top and bottom half which could be opened separately.

Unpacking my small suitcase, the chocolates I hadn't had time to eat spilt out onto the floor. As I knelt to retrieve them, there was a knock on the door.

'Yes?' I said, unable to contain the irritation in my voice.

When there was no answer, I reached up from my kneeling position and pushed open the top half of the door.

It was a local burgher, the man in charge. He simply wanted to know if I needed anything, but I could see that he was also curious about me since I was not from those parts.

I dismissed him more brusquely than I had intended, without even bothering to stand. I needed to be on my own to try to make sense of the fact that earlier that day I had stolen the chocolates from an old street vendor. I had pocketed them while he was distracted by an elegantly-dressed woman examining his pretty, but worthless trinkets. When she saw over the vendor's shoulder what I was doing, I put one finger to my lips and winked, but this did nothing to alleviate her look of horror.

American in Rome

My *permesso di soggiorno* was due to expire. Since I was no longer married to an Italian woman, would I have permission to stay in Rome after living there for ten years? I was wondering about this as I watched the new pope address a small crowd in the piazza. Perhaps if I were granted an audience with him, he could swing the decision in my favour. At the end of the sermon, I raised my hand and stepped forward out of the crowd. Seeing that I was not from those parts, he asked where I was from and what religion I practiced. I confessed that I was 'more of a humanist than anything else', though I occasionally attended Quaker meetings. He listened patiently, but couldn't help smiling at the word 'Quaker'.

That evening I found that I had indeed been granted permission to stay, and went to a fair to celebrate. As it happened, the pope was there too, giving his sermon in a large tent. He waved when he saw me and asked if I would like to contribute something to the gathering. Someone handed me a microphone. Without thinking, I burst into Elvis's All Shook Up: 'A-well-a bless-a ma soul, a-what's a wrong with me...' Everyone turned and stared until the pope began to clap along and sway from side to side. Soon the whole crowd was clapping in time while I sang. I felt a tap on my shoulder. It was my ex-wife.

'You haven't changed much,' she shouted. Her eyes were half-disapproving, half-affectionate,

No, I suppose not, I thought, and wondered if I could ask her to make love to me for old time's sake.

Ends

The poet P., who was a drifter and relied on other people for a place to sleep, came to stay with my mother. When I showed him the poetry collections of his I had kept since my youth, including his very first pamphlet, *Underwater Wedding*, he was moved to tears.

I suggested we go into town to visit an ancient bookshop I knew of. While we waited for the bus, he said a prayer for us both. Then he opened his eyes and saw the expression on my face, and realised I was a non-believer. He prayed that the light of Jesus would come into my life. More than anything, I was worried I had offended him. Although I loved his poetry with its messages in stanza and rhyme, my own prose poems were different. They taught nothing at all. Perhaps my missing faith was no more than a failure of form.

New York Hotel

In the lobby by the revolving glass doors was an old man dressed like Gene Kelly and crooning 'Singing in the Rain' without any musical accompaniment. His voice was frail, but this only served to give the song an added poignancy. Yet no one stopped to listen, or to watch his surprisingly deft tap dance.

After dropping a couple of coins into a hat at the end of the song, I asked him why he was doing this. He told me he had come to the city to look for work more than fifty years ago. While waiting in the lobby by these same doors to speak to someone about a job as a porter, he had started singing popular songs of the day to himself. The hotel owner had happened to pass by in that moment.

'You've got a great voice, kid,' the owner said, taking a puff on his cigar. 'I'll pay you a dollar a day just to stand here and do what you're doing now.'

That old owner was long since dead and the pay had never gone above a dollar a day. Nevertheless, with leftover food from the kitchen, an attic room in the hotel, and with a few tips, he got by.

I wondered why with such a voice he had never tried his hand at getting a record deal. 'I often thought of it,' he said, 'but at first I was afraid of appearing ungrateful to the man who offered me this work when I was down on my luck. Then the years passed more quickly than I thought they would. Now I have no choice except to keep singing here until I'm done. And now if you will excuse me...'

He cleared his throat, spread his arms, and gave everything he had to another song no one had time to listen to.

Capitalists

Our American host invited us to join him for a steak in the restaurant on the top floor of the hotel. There was a great view over the bay and hills of the city, he told us. But a fat British man said he knew of a better place where you could get sea bass.

'I would prefer steak,' I said. 'I don't much care for sea bass.'

'You don't much care for sea bass!' he spluttered, looking me up and down with such contempt that I felt for a moment it was I who had committed the faux pas, not him.

'Well, it's not that I don't like it,' I said weakly. 'It's just that I think steak would be a better idea right now.' I was hoping he would pick up on my hint that it would be a discourtesy to our American host to refuse his invitation.

In any case, none of the lifts of the hotel seemed to be working. One just went straight down to the underground floor, another went up a few feet only to shudder back down again to the floor where we were standing, while a third wouldn't move at all. We were too frightened of doing ourselves an injury to try a fourth. The lifts acted as a kind of leveller and put an end to our quarrel.

Mistake

While I was standing on the Warsaw bridge, a group of Americans stopped and asked me the way to the forest outside the city where the Polish partisans had fought a famous battle. I pointed them in the direction across the river, but warned them it was easy to get lost.

'I'm sure there's no great forest,' said the largest of the Americans, 'only a small wood.'

'Just look on the map,' I said, pointing to the one that was open in his hands. 'Look at all that green – what on earth do you think it is?'

They all gathered round the map and stared at it dubiously.

'I used to cycle on a trail there with my girlfriend,' I told them, 'before my bicycle was stolen one day when we were making love, thinking we were safely hidden in the trees.'

Boardroom Meeting

It was held in a Japanese-style dining room with floor cushions to sit on at a low rectangular table. This was meant to put us at our ease but none of us ever was. Whenever our American boss lost his temper, his huge belly would burst out through the buttons of his white silk shirt and shake like crazy. I did my best to please him and, for good measure, to ingratiate myself with his plump secretary, who sometimes took me into her bed, though this never stopped her from reprimanding me in public for my incompetence in business matters.

Cottage

I wanted to reach the top of the gently sloping hill to see what the view would be on the other side. It meant walking through someone's garden, so I went to knock on their door to ask permission. But the door was already open and no one answered my call. Seeing the stone floor and all the ancient bric-à-brac, I couldn't resist taking a peek around.

A room upstairs with a sloping ceiling clearly belonged to a young girl. It made me nostalgic for my own childhood. Feeling tired, I even lay down like Goldilocks on the small bed in the corner, though my feet dangled over the edge.

I was just falling asleep when I heard someone coming up the stairs. I tried to scramble to my feet, but it was too late. A woman was standing in the doorway with a brush and pan. I tried to think of an explanation, but then I saw that she didn't expect any.

'Good morning,' she said, and began sweeping the floor.

When I went down into the hallway, backpackers were milling around just outside. I realised that I was in a guesthouse. I left through the back entrance and continued my journey up the hill. Near the top were half a dozen middle-aged women sun-bathing. They were all giggling and pointing at a zebra, or rather two men dressed as a zebra, performing somersaults down the slope.

Someone touched my elbow. It was an old school friend I hadn't seen for decades. 'Ah, there you are,' she said. 'I've been looking for you.' Her hair was long and brown as it had been when we were teenagers.

Married

I was so hungry going back down the hill that I stopped and asked a family picnicking if I could have a bit of their picnic. 'Sure,' the dad said, but there was nothing left in the hamper, and so I helped myself to bits from his children's paper plates, indeed too many bits to be within the bounds of decency. The dad started to look nervous. Was I some kind of maniac? If only my wife were with me, I thought, he would see that I am really a good man. It's just that I have got lost trying to find my way home.

Vertigo

'Caterpillars become butterflies, but crows become frogs,' she said, 'because they croak so much and fly too close to the ground.' She had led me onto a slippery wet slope, which dropped away to a sheer cliff. The crows swooped over our heads, and I felt dizzy when I looked down. 'Come on,' she said, offering her hand. I was too afraid to move, so she went on her way without me.

Waves

People were huddled in the doorway, waiting their turn to speak to her. She sat opposite me at a small table. It was a place where you could go if you needed someone to talk to – a small hall made from the hull of an upturned boat. To emphasise my troubles, every now and then I reached over and gently jabbed her. She must have been used to people like me. She smiled and listened. Her breasts rose and fell with each breath like the sea.

When I Was Eight

Walking in the fields, I saw a lone Alsatian dog. It started running towards me. I thought the safest thing would be to lie down, to close my eyes and feign dead. A moment later, flat on the ground, I felt the dog sniffing and nuzzling my face. Then I felt its teeth around my wrist, but the dog was not biting me. It was trying to pull me towards something.

I opened my eyes. A man with a farmer's cap was bending over me. 'My dog's a bit worried about you,' he said. 'Why don't you throw a stick for him? He only wants to be your friend.'

Hollywood

I got a deal with him to write a script. He had produced *Lassie* and other famous films back in the 1940s. My wife came with me to meet him in a Hollywood café. We had to go through a field full of sheep guarded by a collie whose master had recently died. I knew she could turn nasty if you didn't have the knack of handling her.

At the café we sat with the film producer and I began talking about my plans for the script. But instead of listening to me, he was soon flirting with my wife. She seemed quite happy to go along with him. I told them both to go to hell, tore up the contract I had been given to sign, and walked out.

The collie was waiting for me outside the café. My wife and the film producer would come to regret their behaviour when they saw how I could make her love me.

Orphanage

It was my responsibility to accompany the boy in a taxi to an orphanage on the other side of the city. When we arrived, I was surprised to see what a rundown area it was in. I wondered if we had come to the right place. Although I was worried about the expense, I told the driver to wait while I took the boy and went to find out.

An old man who looked like a butler from a bygone age answered the door. He led us into a deserted table tennis room. 'Wait here,' he said.

We waited for what seemed ages. It grew dark. I pressed the light switch, but after a brief flicker the bulb went out.

I took the boy's hand. 'Let's get out of here,' I said.

But I couldn't find the way out. By this time the boy was weeping loudly. Through a corridor window, I could see the taxi driver taking a call on his mobile. Then, with a shrug of his shoulders, he drove away.

Assistance

It was the last tube train I could get home. I had coins with me for a ticket, but the machine was jammed. The lady at the kiosk told me she couldn't sell me a ticket since it was no longer in her job description to do so. How would I get through the barrier at the other end without a ticket? I asked her. With a sigh, she came out of the kiosk and walked over to me. She stood so close I could smell her hair and feel the warmth of her skin. That was enough to comfort me for the fact that nothing could be done with the machine.

Conditions

I moved back to Paris for a job teaching English. My first evening there I met up with an old friend in a McDonald's. Rather a strange choice of place on his part, I thought, but since it was his treat I said nothing. He insisted we have the special deal: a Big Mac and a glass of red wine for seven euros. The Big Macs took a long time in coming, and my friend started to get impatient. After all these years of not seeing each other we had little in common. I was looking forward to escaping and crashing out in the teachers' flat, however cramped and dusty it was.

The next morning I was a passenger in a car driven by another new teacher, Nia Z. She got lost and ended by going up a boulevard the wrong way into oncoming traffic. She got away with it because of her Welsh good looks. To think we had only come out to buy some fresh milk for breakfast! Her French lover had left the milk on the table all night instead of putting it back in the fridge.

Foursome

The TV reality show specialised in cruel practices to see how victims and the audience would react. Anything vulnerable was a target, even a family of mice nesting in a hole in a block of wood in a waste ground behind some flats. I caught the perpetrator in the act when he was about to set fire to the nest.

'I've had an unhappy childhood,' he said. 'This is my way of making up for it.'

'I've had an unhappy life too,' I said, 'but it hasn't led to me doing such things.'

This was not true. I had been cruel in my own way, and my life had not always been an unhappy one, only at times, mainly when as a child I had been frightened of other children each time I moved school, or when I had been lonely living in foreign cities, where my only source of comfort had been the seduction (and abandonment) of women, many of whom I did not even feel attracted to. Once by mistake I made a date with two women on the same night. I was saved by an old colleague, whom I hadn't seen for years, who happened to turn up at my flat, which was at the top of a narrow spiral staircase, and which was cluttered with my landlord's ancient and dusty furniture.

Polished

Cycling through the city centre of Turin, I stopped off at a bar for a coffee. It was a much more elegant place than I had taken it to be from the outside. In fact, it was not really a bar at all, but a kind of salon which looked as if it had hardly changed since the 1890s. The waiter courteously led me to a hallway (just as elegant) where I could leave my bike. Inside the salon, I recognised an old British friend with a group of smart Italians drinking aperitifs. He nodded to me, but did not invite me to join them, so I sat on my own at a tiny antique table.

I was going to leave a tip of one euro when my friend beckoned me over. I had to bend down so that he could whisper in my ear: 'Five euros are the very least you should leave, or you'll make us both cut a poor figure.'

Smoke

I bumped into Gerald R. near the centre of Turin, just outside the college where I was working. He had kept his long hair and beard, though they were now matted and streaked with white. Shouting to make myself heard above the traffic, I asked after his wife (whose name I couldn't remember) and daughter, Laura. He said she was being treated for depression, but I didn't know whether he was referring to his wife or daughter. The latter I remembered as a lively and curious toddler. The Italian doctors weren't much use when it came to mental illness, he told me, taking the cigarette I offered and sucking furiously as if that were now the most important thing in the world.

It struck me just how long we had been living abroad. I was only here by chance. I had met Gerald in a bar years before when I was on my way to the station after a backpacking tour. It was he who had told me about the college job. Somewhere I still had my unused return train ticket to England. I wondered absurdly if it might still be valid.

I felt a soft punch on my shoulder. Gerald wanted to know if I could spare him another cigarette.

Promise

I went into the Turin bookshop where Carlo Castiglione worked. He had just published his first novel with a small independent press. It was a book I admired. I introduced myself and asked him if anyone was translating his book into English. If not, would he be interested in me doing the translation? He was full of enthusiasm over the idea, and I promised I would be back to talk about it.

I never returned. Perhaps I was simply envious that he had written the novel I always wanted to write.

A few years later I caught sight of him outside Porta Nuova station. By this time he was a famous author with his books translated into several languages. I did not think he would notice me in the crowd, but as he passed, his eye caught mine, and he seemed to be on the verge of greeting me. I hurried on towards my waiting train, yet couldn't resist turning a few moments later to watch him walk away from the station and into the city I was leaving behind.

3

Free Will

'Come on,' the youth said, running towards me. He grabbed my hand and I found myself running too, straight towards a wall so that I had no choice than to jump with him. On the other side was a drop of several feet. We both fell onto our backs, but to my surprise, although I was winded, the only part of me that hurt was my foot. It had caught on a precious vase on the top of the wall. The youth was doubled up, not with pain, but with laughter. He took hold of my hand again.

'You'll have to pay for that smashed vase,' he told me.

'But the jump was your idea.'

'It was your foot,' he said, and gripped my hand even tighter.

Responsibilities

When I came back to our hotel room, I found the bell-boy kissing my wife's naked shoulder. He looked at me without apology, almost as if he expected *me* to apologise for interrupting *him*. I walked out of the room, down the stairs and out into the street. I kept walking. In my left hand, I had the present I had just bought for my wife's birthday, in my right the keys to the room. What was I supposed to do with them now?

Resistance

I lived in Turin with my Italian wife. Her father, who was half-paralysed after being knocked down by a van, lived a few streets away. He was in agonising pain most of the time. One day I caught my wife deliberately rubbing salt into the sores on his stomach. He was helpless to stop her, yet too ashamed of his daughter's behaviour to cry out.

I used to go and visit him on my old moped. It was slow and wobbly, and made other drivers on the narrow streets so impatient they would come close to running over pedestrians in their hurry to overtake me.

Relations

When I went back to our flat in Turin for the first time in ages, I found it was occupied by all kinds of people I had never seen before, but who claimed to be related to my Italian wife. They were talking about how they were going to sell the flat. It seemed that they had forgotten it belonged to my wife and me.

I had come mainly to pick up the translation I had done of Pierre Reverdy's *Le Voleur de Talan*. It took me a while to find it amongst all the things that were now strewn around the place. I decided to leave as soon as I could on the night train from Turin to Paris to deliver it to Reverdy's editor there.

His office was closed when I arrived the next morning. I went into a bar next door and ordered a coffee. The waitress shrugged when I asked her if she knew when the office would open. I hoped her demeanour would become a little more deferential when I showed her my manuscript, but her attention was now turned to a crowd of people coming through the swinging doors – my wife's family from Italy. They must have followed me all the way to Paris, perhaps with the intention of seeing what financial gain could be made, or more likely out of a sense of sheer gossipy interest in my life, which they would never understand.

Ex

N. came to a conference at the university where I worked. She had written an academic paper in Italian. My British colleagues were doubtful about its merits just because it was not written in English. I told them that as it happened, she and I had once been married and I knew the paper would be brilliant. You could see this, in fact, simply by glancing at her handwriting and detailed illustrations, which looked as if they came from an ancient manuscript. I would translate it for them, though my translation could never be as beautiful as the original, just as the love I had shown her never truly reflected the love I felt within.

License

When I was 30, I phoned my old girlfriend from Turin and eventually met up with her when I moved back there for a few months. She was a little mistrustful at first – and her mother was dead against me – but soon it was like the old days before we had split up. Then my job came to an end. I went back to England, met someone else and we lost touch.

Many years later, after my divorce, I got in contact with her again. Her mother was no longer alive and she agreed to see me. We went for a walk in the hills where she had once driven me in her first car and got stuck on a steep slope. I hadn't been able to help her because I didn't know how to drive. At least now I had my driver's license

Left Open

The poet from India was over eighty years old, but still full of youthful enthusiasm. I had arranged for him to come and talk to my students. On the day he arrived, however, I couldn't stay with him in the lecture hall because I needed to return home to have the lock on my back door fixed. I introduced him to the students, apologised for having to leave, and said that I hoped to invite another poet, my father, for next term's lecture. Then I remembered that my father was dead. 'Sorry about that,' I said. The students giggled – they all thought it was a joke, part of the show.

The poet said that he had known my father back in the day. I felt the hint of a reproach in this, as if it was something I had failed to acknowledge. The students waited for my reply, but what I had to say was not for their ears. Besides, I had to get away to meet the man who was going to sort out my door.

Adult College

The fat student was weeping because I had forgotten to turn up for his individual tutorial. He blurted out that this was the story of his life. I told him I was so busy I had forgotten all kinds of things recently, even my own daughter's birthday. I knelt down – by this time he had collapsed onto the floor of the corridor and a small crowd was gathered around us – and put my hand on his quivering shoulder. But this only made him cry all the more, and twist and turn like a baby in its cot.

Preserve

I was in Paris to put the final touches to my book on Pierre Reverdy. The poet Maurice X welcomed me into his apartment, but it soon became apparent that he was more interested in having sex with me than in giving advice, though we were both old men. He was ill with cancer, he told me, and wanted to get the most out of life while he still could. I left with most of my questions unanswered.

Then there was the critic, Jérôme Y. I had his address, but no phone number, and the print on my map was so tiny I couldn't find his street. Besides, he might not welcome me turning up unannounced at his door.

I wondered about my ex, Simone. It was she who had introduced me to the work of Reverdy, but I didn't even know if she was still alive. In any case, what would she say if she saw me now? I remembered the way she used to run a finger along each of my ribs and then down over my stomach to the inside of my thighs, whispering that if she were a sculptor, she would make a statue of me to keep me whole.

History

The French woman at the picnic table wouldn't stop talking. She seemed crazy with grief, and I felt I had no choice but to listen. Another man at the table kept watching me out of the corner of his eye, as if I were harbouring some dishonourable intention. Perhaps he thought I wanted to seduce her, but nothing could have been further from my mind – she was all skin and bone, her prematurely grey hair tied too tight in a lifeless pony tail. The man by contrast was portly and pompous-looking. A ring of beer foam was stuck to his moustache.

'Don't worry,' he broke in, 'you can speak French to me. I understand French.' She looked at him as if he were now the one who could rescue her.

'Moi aussi,' I protested, 'moi aussi. Je parlais en anglais avec vous simplement parce que vous –'

Here I stopped because I could not remember how to conjugate the verb. In any case, I had an excuse not to continue for at that moment a military parade appeared at the end of the street. It was led by a general in a jeep. When he saw us at the table, he stood and shouted for all he was worth about the need for everyone to be mobilised, man and woman, old and young. The time for our sloppy private concerns was over.

Volunteer

We were all in a large tent. Sitting at untidily laid-out trestle tables, we had to sort out hundreds of letters, stick labels with addresses on envelopes, put the letters inside and seal them with a lick. I was surprised at how quickly my mouth and tongue got sore. I had come in good faith, but was now wondering how I could escape.

A tall American lady dressed in a red uniform seemed to be standing guard at the flap door. She wanted to know why I was leaving so soon. Before I could reply, she pointed to the ring on my finger. 'Oh,' she said, 'the best ones always get taken, don't they?' She gave me a bundle of large letters and envelopes to take home with me, to make sure I was kept busy and useful.

Subversive

I had defied the state. Now arrest was imminent. I wondered where to hide my exercise books, which were full of subversive thoughts. I wished I had hidden them sooner. Eventually, I found a place to put them under some folded sheets in my mother's airing cupboard. I decided to go for an early morning walk – it might be the last chance I had to enjoy any freedom. It was a sunny day. People nodded hello but did not stop to chat as they usually did. Word had obviously got around about my arrest. I thought about the exercise books – the place I had hidden them in was hopelessly inadequate. The agents would turn my mother's house upside down. However, I doubted whether there was time to hide them anywhere else. All I could do now was live each moment of this morning.

Caught

My wife showed the film they'd made of me. What surprised me was the thinness of my hair, its straggly wildness, but more than that the crazy look of desire in my eyes as I stared at the woman I was dancing with, whose name I didn't know.

Smooch

The ancient dwarf lady played a video she'd made of her romancing with David Cameron, to the accompaniment of 1950s doo-wop songs. It was all spliced together – a film collage. She'd never met David C. Nevertheless, the video made for compelling viewing. It showed them at a fair together on the big wheel, going up and down, round and round, waving and smiling like royalty, egged on by the cheers of the crowd who had gathered to watch.

Ruse

We arrived too early at the airport to check in. Although it was busy, we managed to find a place on a long seat in a passageway, which formed a bridge between the car park and the departures lounge. My wife took out some photos to show us. We huddled round them. It felt like a rare family moment. Normally we were so busy there seemed to be no time just to sit together. We didn't notice our suitcase was sticking out so that people had to squeeze round. A bunch of young men, who looked like soldiers in civvies, pushed by us. One of them swore and wondered out loud why our suitcase was blocking the way. As soon as I could, I got up to move it, but the suitcase was no longer there. The men must have taken it. Perhaps their behaviour had simply been a ruse to steal from us. Then I saw them through the window. They were in a passageway on a bridge parallel to ours, laughing and shoving their way through the crowd.

Resources

There had been a misunderstanding. Halfway through our cheap holiday we were informed at midnight that we would have to check out of our hotel the next morning. When I woke, there was an even longer queue than usual for the shower. By the time I got to the cubicle, it was filthy. A fat man was staring at me through the cubicle glass while he waited his turn. Why did his eyes follow my every attempt to wash myself with the last bit of soap remaining?

If only I had been quicker getting into the queue. It was likely now that no rooms would be available anywhere apart from the slum at the edge of town. We would have to walk under the sun with our suitcases all the way along the packed beach to get there. Even if we found a room, it might mean sharing with penniless strangers. And here I was still in the shower, wasting time.

Rogues

The elephant chased us through the forest. Did it really bear us malice, or was it just curious?

We came to a rock face, impossible to climb. I turned, picked up a log and swung it to scare the elephant away. Instead, it reached its trunk towards us, almost tenderly.

I grabbed my wife's hand. We ducked around the elephant and ran up a hill between close-set trees.

On the other side was a deserted mansion. But now a bunch of locals was after us. Were they cops or criminals?

They were nearly at the door of an old dining hall where we were hiding. We climbed up onto a wide, tall cupboard in the corner, convinced we would not be found. Then we heard a ladder being put against the cupboard and a moment later a small torch was shone in our faces. But the torch was held by a woman with a kind face. She looked as if she had discovered two naughty children, rather than a bewildered, middle-aged couple.

4

Putin's English Tutor

On my way to work, I avoid the small number of people demonstrating for freedom. They have my sympathy, but I don't want to be arrested by the police, beaten up by fascist street thugs, or lose my well-paid job. Besides, Putin has his ways to make me love him. As we walk down the palace corridor together towards his office suite, he puts his arm around me affectionately like a father. The Russians are on our side in the fight against the terrorists, he says in that soft voice of his. Before we part, he throws his arms around me Russian-style. His embrace is so tight it might be a bear hug. He brings me to the verge of tears.

Recall

Tony Blair has dyed his hair light brown and grown it all the way to his shoulders. Instead of a tie, he is wearing a collarless shirt. Gone is the haggard look. He is almost his old hippy self. Each time he is asked an awkward question about where his government went wrong with its international policies, he shrugs, smiles sheepishly and admits he 'didn't get everything right'. His friend Alistair has grown his hair long again, too. He sits nearby, head down like a moody teenager. Every now and again, he exchanges a wink with Tony.

My Involvement

First I was on the American plane that dropped its bomb on Hiroshima. I was there purely to be a witness to the event as it unfolded in true technicolour, someone who would never forget the brightness of the orange fires.

Then I was on the ground trying to hide in the jungle from Japanese troops. They were everywhere. I hid in a concrete pipe where I thought no one would find me, but I was discovered by some Japanese children. They regarded me with a strange, yet tender curiosity, and then with a series of quick motions beckoned me to follow them.

They led me by a secret path back to a school on the outskirts of the city. It was one of the few buildings still intact. An elegant woman, who must have been the children's teacher, let me inside. A few moments later there was a banging on the door. The woman ushered me into a dining room, and pointed to a table covered by a brocaded tablecloth of flame-like orange, under which I hid as the troops stormed in.

Accident

When the war was over, the railways reopened and I took a train to the sea. A lot of other people had the same idea, and soon the train was packed. I got up to let someone else sit down and hung onto a strap. A little further down the carriage, I recognised the fireman who lived down the street from me. I nodded hello and he mouthed something, but I couldn't make out what it was, so squeezed my way down the carriage towards him. Then a sudden slowing of the train threw me right against him. He shrank away with a horrified expression, as if I'd done it on purpose. To try to put him at ease, I told him I was looking forward to some peace and quiet by the sea. He looked at me as if I was mad.

When the train arrived, the tightness of the crowd meant we had to stay together until we reached the town centre. Here there was a celebratory parade of the Fire Brigade with its magnificent engines. At risk of life and limb, the fireman dashed to the other side of the street just to get away from me.

Kiss

When I saw her in the market place, I remembered her room with its posters of Marc Bolan and how soft her lips had been when we sat on her narrow bed and kissed all those years ago. I remembered her brother who worked one summer on a chicken battery farm. The hens never suffered, he told me. They were too stupid. You could put your foot on a hen's backside and it would think you were a cock.

I was still a virgin and I think he was too, but neither of us was going to tell the other. His sister would sit on the bed with me, but never lie down. Would she recognise me now?

Early Retirement

After many years abroad, I moved to a small village in Cornwall. The locals immediately took to me because I seemed foreign and exotic. The plump, middle-aged woman at the Post Office asked me if I would take on the leading male role in a production that was going to be put on at the village hall. She would play the leading lady. I was too ashamed to admit that I wouldn't be able to remember the lines. Instead I told her my schedule was already packed, mumbling a lie about a book to write. She blushed as if I'd slapped her. Perhaps another year, I suggested, though I knew my memory would be even worse by then. She shook her head. My standing in the community would never be the same again.

Investigations

'Don't you remember how beautiful the girls were?'

I was speaking to my old school friend, who used to write love poems and read philosophy. He said nothing, only frowned in melancholy fashion.

'But don't you remember how crazy we were about Daryl Cooke? The liquid look in her brown almond eyes, the sun on the waves of hair down her shoulders, the green school skirt tight around her bum! What did we care about the odd blackhead on her nose!'

My friend could have put this much better, but he remained silent, his thoughts somewhere else entirely.

'I wonder what she looks like now. I bet she is even more beautiful.' As I said this, I realised I was imagining a woman in her early thirties, forgetting that it was nearly five decades since I had last seen her.

'And philosophy,' I said. 'Do you remember how you made me read Wittgenstein, and how I struggled with him?'

For a moment, a light came into his eyes. 'Of course,' he said. And in his voice was still a trace of the pomposity of the adolescent trying to sound much older and wiser than he is.

Debts

Back in Paris on business, I paid a surprise visit to my old friend Pierre. I thought he would greet me warmly but he was strangely reserved. It turned out that since his father died, he no longer had any money and was behind with the rent. In my youth his family had been more than generous with me and now he wanted me to return the kindness. Before I could reply, there was a knock on the door. The huge-bellied landlord, with a couple of henchmen at his side, demanded that I pay the arrears. I told him I didn't have that kind of money, but both of us knew it wasn't true. He asked me to meet him later in rue X near the station and to bring along a suitcase of cash. When I got there, I saw it wasn't a 'rue' at all, but a boulevard, as I pointed out to him, because it consisted of wide lanes on either side of a strip of grass, which was dying, as I also pointed out to him, due to all the traffic fumes.

The Killer

Jerry Lee Lewis has aged. No longer does he swagger and fool around as he did in the old days, like the night I saw him playing country boogie-woogie on a grand piano in a posh French restaurant. I remember how he jumped up onto the piano and played it with his feet, the notes still melodious.

It was my friend Bob who took me to that restaurant on the night. He eats and drinks there several times a week even now. He is treated like an aristocrat by the waiters, who address him as 'Monsieur Bob'. But where does he get the money from? He retired years ago – he doesn't have time to work, he says. Although he has grown fat, he somehow looks good, unlike the bloated JLL, who can hardly move, but who still insists on playing the piano with his arthritic hands, sitting in a wheelchair, the music as beautiful as ever.

Reckoning

The blues festival would soon be under way. A woman with long, dyed red hair sat next to me in the auditorium. She looked familiar, but I couldn't quite place her.

'You don't know who I am,' she said, as if she expected as much.

Was she someone I had once slept with? Was she someone I owed money to? 'I'm sorry –'

She gave me a note written on an old scrap of paper. It was from a friend I had lost touch with years ago. In a tiny handwriting full of crossings out, there was a list of things that he had done for me and another list of things that I had done for him. The second list was much shorter.

'Perhaps my old friend should pay more attention to his own shortcomings,' I said to the woman. 'He always said he would be a famous blues singer, but no one has heard of him.'

'Just wait for the show to begin,' she said. In her pale blue eyes (ill-matched to the dyed red hair), was a glint I recognised.

Festival

The stage was huge, so I moved around as much as I could to stop it from looking so empty. I was singing Elvis to an audience in a park that stretched away as far as the eye could see. When I had done my turn, I went into the makeshift bar in a tent at the back of the stage. An old pal of mine – who had kept his hair long from our heyday together, though it was now grey and straggly – was getting drunk as usual. I tried to take the bottle from his hand, which everyone at the bar found both touching and uproarious. A true friend, one of them laughed.

There was a sudden stink of piss. A toilet had overflowed and piss was coming into the tent. I was terrified of stepping into it on my way back to the stage for my second turn. My pal offered me a slug of his drink to steady my nerves. One drink led to another. By the time I got onto the stage, it was pitch black in the park, and everything had gone quiet. I had no idea if anyone was still out there to hear me sing songs into the night in a voice that was not my own.

Loved

I came across Priscilla's young daughter wandering through the park on her own. She was half-carrying, half-dragging a large doll by one of its hands. The doll reminded me of her late father, with his stiff, dyed-black hair and dark eye shadow. I had seen him once in concert in 1970. I remembered him walking through the audience full of gratitude as if he himself could not believe that he was there, singing better than he ever had. How could we have known that he would soon no longer care whether he lived or died?

I found Priscilla weeping on a bench. She waved me away without even looking up. It was people like me who through our adoration had killed her loved one, she shouted after me.

Country

I was always hanging around the same place, the *Bar Italia*, hoping something would come up – a job, an adventure, or a sexual liaison. The barman offered me some medicines he had under the counter. They would never give you these at the chemist's, he said.

He was right. They made me feel better. I went to call my mother from the bar's phone-booth. The English dialling tone started even before I had put in my *gettoni;* something must have gone wrong with the phone, but this meant I could talk to my mother for free, though I had no idea what it was I was going to say. A queue – or rather, since this was Italy, a small crowd – started to build behind me. There were murmurs of discontent – why was I taking over the only phone in the bar, and one of the very few phones in town? So I had an excuse to hang up.

I went back to my little round table, and sat down to take some more medicine with my *espresso*. But it made me sad that I had not talked to my mother, and I glanced over at the phone booth to see how long I would have to wait before I could call again. To my surprise, the booth was empty. They had not been waiting to use the phone at all. They were simply resentful because I was a foreigner.

An expat friend wandered in. He was in a similar position to me, but older. We spent the whole day together, switching from coffee to red wine in the afternoon. I was more optimistic than he was, but if I'd had any sense I would have taken a long look at my companion and realised what awaited me unless I did something to change my life. He kept loading the same country song over and over again onto the jukebox until the barman told him to stop.

Lightning Source UK Ltd.
Milton Keynes UK
UKHW01f0628260718
326318UK00001B/252/P